Elusive

Poems of Joy, Sorrow, Light and Love

By Jerry Caspell

Elusive Butterfly

Poems of Joy, Sorrow, Light and Love

By Jerry Caspell

Shoestring Book Publishing

Elusive Butterfly

Paperback

ISBN: 978-1-496123589

Published by;
Shoestring Book Publishing.

For information address;
shoestringpublishing4u@gmail.com

Table of Contents

Preface viii

elusive butterfly 1

Sad And Lonely 2

Please Tell Me 4

Stardust Light and Love 6

Angel of Light 7

destiny 8

The Twilight Hours 10

Endless Moment 11

My Stylist 12

The Paradox 14

This Pain 16

Stay in Bed 18

Escape 19

Your Dwelling Place 20

We Poets 22

Broken Soul 23

Passion 24

Life is Good 26

I Need a Fix 27

The Key 28

Shadow Boxing 30

Enigma 32

Winter's Chill 33

Of Lonely Souls 34

airborne virus 36

Spadina Street 37

Author's note: 37

The Fire of Life 38

illusion 40

Losing You 41

A Place of Peace 42

Storms 44

Wayward Soul 45

In My Dream 46

If Only 48

solitude and silence 49

Huggers of the Soul 50

I'm Here 51

I Love My Life 52

Prolific 54

Lock the Door 56

Something About You 57

Catharsis of Poetry 58

Sunny Rain 59

The Truth of Me 60

Kindred Soul 62

One Desire 64

Blissful Butterfly 65

Sometimes Sadness 66

Frozen Emotion 67

soul flowers 68

my life 69

Sorrow Floats 70

Tempests 71

Tormented Soul 72

Soul Quake 73

uninspired 74

My Year of Tears 75

Drifting 76

Author's Biography 79

Preface

Poetry, for me, seemed to come naturally, since I was a teenager.

It has been a very personal and private expression of my deepest feelings and longings, and a means of self-discovery. I seldom shared what was so personal with anyone. But from time to time I would find someone who expressed an interest in my poetry and I'd be willing to let them have a look. Such a person is my most amazing and inspiring friend, Anna Moses, who became the main motivating force to change my mind about sharing my poetry. Originally from Russia, Anna told me of famous Russian poets like Pushkin and Lermontov, and would provide me translations of their poems. She once told me I seemed to write with the soul of such poets, often expressing sadness, despair and the pain of the world. That really resonated within me because I so often find a sense of fulfillment and peace as I write about my sadness and sorrow, along with joy and love. My poetry always seems to have a deeply personal cathartic effect. Anna first encouraged me to find a group or website where I could share my poetry; always helping, advising and encouraging me every step of the way. Anna is the reason I am publishing my first book, and she is much more than my most amazing and wonderful friend; she is obviously my Muse:

Floating on the wind,

A feather soul ...

Tossed to and fro ... drifting,

Lifting high, sinking low,

Aimless, lost ...

At the mercy of the breeze.

And yet this feather soul believes,

an end to loneliness this leads,

Another feather soul floats by,

Entangled, we sigh ...

Entwined, we find ...

Our hearts at ease ...

Circumstance or chance,

Or Divine design brings peace

And joyous news ...

I've found my Muse

My book "Elusive Butterfly" is an expression of my deepest emotions:
from sadness, sorrow and pain, to love, happiness and joy. I hope you
will discover your own soul in the midst of these poems, or perhaps
you can relate to my feelings and find beauty in sadness, music in
love and inspiration in the mystery.

Jerry

elusive butterfly

elusive butterfly

flutters by

delicate and shy

when I reached for her

she flew high

far above, beyond my grasp

so why try

yet in quiet calm and stillness

another time, another day

she came my way

she chose to land upon my shoulder

this is the way of happiness

we cannot catch or hold her

wait patiently and see

she will find you and me

don't ask me why

she is an elusive butterfly

Sad And Lonely

I awaken sad and lonely

With emptiness and pain

An aching void inside me

The crying seems in vain

Is there no end to sorrow

No ceasing of despair

Is there no hope tomorrow

No laughter anywhere

No caring arms to hold me

To soothe away my tears

No sacred wings enfold me

To chase away my fears

And what I thought was joy before

And all that I called love

Was false and shallow, nothing more

The Phantom's mask and glove

And I awaken sad and lonely

Gladness and joy have flown

Peace is a stranger to me

I feel so alone

Please Tell Me

How do you soothe your sorrow

As it rushes through your soul

Do you send it to tomorrow

Or bury it in a hole

Inside the deep recesses

Of the corners of your mind

Or smother it with caresses

From anyone you can find

Who feels the common feeling

And needs your comfort too

Sweet kisses bringing healing

To the pain inside of you

So many ways we keep on trying

To push away our pain

And ease the endless crying

This throbbing in our brain

Is a voice inside replying

Before you go insane

Where do you put your sadness

When it just won't go away

Do you wear a mask of gladness

Fall on your knees and pray

Oh please tell me, I'm begging you

To ease this cruel fate, don't hesitate

I need to know,

Please tell me what to do ...

Perhaps it won't be too late

For me to try it too

And I'm the kind of guy

Who will do the same for you

Stardust Light and Love

If I could I'd carry your sorrow,
  Far beyond the stars
Your memories of pain I'd borrow,
  Bury them all on Mars

Your tears of torment and despair,
  I'd hurl them into space
They would all dissolve and disappear,
  Every mournful cry erased

Then I'd bring back from the heavens,
  Some stardust sparkling bright
Sprinkle it all around you,
  To bathe you in new light

The angel's songs shall follow,
  With joyous melodies
To vanquish every sorrow,
  In endless harmonies

We shall soar the clouds above,
  Upon these songs we'll fly
Riding on wings of love,
  Together, you and I

Angel of Light

A smile that can carry my sorrows away

Enlightens and brightens my dark lonely day

With mystical power to change how I feel

Such whimsical, wonderful, winsome appeal

This radiant countenance vanishes night

An aura so glorious, brilliant and bright

A soft touch to heal my sad soul when it aches

Whispered words always soothing my heart when it breaks

She isn't a dream, she is real as can be

I knew it the moment her wings covered me

She flew from afar and awakened new sight

And only I see her, my Angel of Light

Note:
Inspired by this Bible verse:
Do not neglect to show hospitality to strangers, for
thereby some have entertained angels unawares.

destiny

what sadness do you feel,
what fears weigh you down,
what gladness do you bury,
as your exhausted hopes drown

my sorrow seems to smother my soul
I wonder if it happens to you
life like a whirlwind, out of control
do you sometimes feel this too

if you could only tell me what you feel
if I could only reach inside your mind
would this bring some comfort or reveal
a truth I cannot seem to find

or would our combined sadness multiply

and bring us further into dark despair

yet being lost together we might try

to heal the common sorrow that we share

my lonely heart is aching, don't you see

can you hear my heart it's breaking constantly

come and open up your lonely heart to me

and together we can change what life can be

perhaps together we can change our destiny

The Twilight Hours

In the twilight hours between night and day

My mind races, myriad images, thoughts abound

In these waking hours my heart embraces

Melodies and memories where only joy is found

Places of endless beauty, the wonders of this world

People of my past who taught me love, I think of them

People in my life today, cherished more than priceless gems

This is the place where dreams are born

Where hope is formed, where life rejoices

Amidst a thousand choices, voices call to me

I am renewed, my deepest desires, passions pursued

Oh to linger here in the twilight hours

Lavished in love in this sacred place

Filled with abundant life and grace

Discovering the true heart of me, my soul made new

Knowing, overflowing with purpose and kindness

And love for someone waiting, anticipating

I awaken to live and give this all to you ...

Endless Moment

One moment is all I need

The hint of a smile as our eyes meet

No words necessary

Thoughts weave a tapestry

Fingers entwine

Grafted vines

Sharing sustenance

Forsaking independence

You are a part of me

A single heart now beats magically

An act of will, or destiny

In one mystical endless moment

We came to be

I in you ...

You in me ...

My Stylist

Lily cut my hair today

She's really the very best

I got the works as they say

Shampoo and all the rest

She has some magic fingers

Rippling through my hair

I think she washed away some pain

Rinsed it right out of there

No pain, my gain ...

Down ...

The ...

Drain ...

Then she snipped away some sorrow

I saw it fall to the floor

I may come back tomorrow

Ask her to take off a little more

If you're down, I recommend Lily

She's got amazing skills

You may think I'm being silly

But she can cure a bunch of ills

The Paradox

How in the midst of despair and pain
Can joy overwhelm, overflow
How when hope seems to all fade away
Can life and happiness grow

What a paradox is this twisted dance
This song with no harmony
So disjointed by every circumstance
Becomes a ballet and symphony

The good and the bad and indifferent
When standing alone bring confusion
But together in a higher, grander scheme
Make sense and dispel all illusion

And the dance of despair and of joy
And the song of woe and elation
Bring a depth and a warmth and a glory
In union a new creation

And the pain and despair make life sweeter

For the joy is enhanced by each woe

And the dance and the song are far better

And love through each sorrow will grow

And while seemingly contradicting

The pain intermingling with joy

Brings a purpose to life and new meaning

And a pleasure that none can destroy

So welcome the sorrow and sadness

And cherish the darkness you fear

For the joys and the pleasures, the hope and the light

Are so very, very near

This Pain

Sadness overwhelms me

Emptiness consuming

Despair is all that's there

Soul-flowers are not blooming

I long to question why

A reason for how I feel

This inner sigh, this cry

This alone seems real

No magic happy potion

This is the way it is

This is my true emotion

This is what my heart says

No pretense, no pretending

No falsehood, no denial

No effort for truth-bending

No thoughts of self-revile

Sometimes I need this pain

I'm giving up the sham

For whether loss or gain

It tells me who I am

Stay in Bed

Gray cold rainy morning
wish I could stay in bed
weather girl issued a warning
clouds in my overcast head

Storm is getting worse
is she talking about outside
or in my cold heart universe
downpour on the inside

It may sound a little insane
or like some terrible transgression
maybe I'm in a higher power brain
and this is Divine depression

A speck in a vast galaxy
miniscule molecule in God's head
everything is so much bigger than me
wish I could stay in bed

Escape

I'm up ... I'm down
I'm laughing, yet I frown ...
... inside. ... I hide
If I had wings I'd fly
Perhaps the wind
... would make the tears dry

Rising above the clouds ...
   beyond, so far, no fear
There is no more down
   outside the atmosphere
No air, I don't care ...
   so high ...
   kiss the world goodbye

Your Dwelling Place

You drifted through my mind today
  a dozen times or more
I'm so glad you visit me this way,
  my soul has an open door

How pleasant are these thoughts of you,
  imagining your smile
my heart cries "forget me not", it's true,
  please linger here a while

The next time that I see you,
  please indulge me as I stare
I'm saving another view of you,
  a memory when you're not there

I will hold your hand the whole night through,
  run my fingers through your hair
all my senses hold a part of you,
  with every moment that we share

As I kiss your luscious lips tonight,
  as I hold you in my arms
I will cling to you with all my might,
  keep you safe from every harm

I need your smell, your tender touch, your taste,
  inside my soul, inside my heart
so you can dwell in me, never be erased,
  and we shall never be apart

We Poets

some people see beyond this veil of sorrow

it is most often from these poets I must borrow

glimmers of hope so I can see

rays of joy, a glimpse into tomorrow

their sunshine lights the way for me

and sometimes, although fleetingly

a spark comes forth from within me too

to bring the gift of happiness to you

it works both ways, we poets know

our words are seeds for souls to grow

sorrow, sadness, hope and joy

everything we feel and express

when hatred only would destroy

we healers of the world's distress

we poets bring forth happiness

Broken Soul

broken soul

shattered heart

a thousand pieces

scattered apart

no more tears

fears remain

silent sadness

piercing pain

fix me

can you

mend me

with soul glue

I'm begging you

Passion

Oh passion where did you go
You left without a trace
And now I'm sighing, crying
My heart is an empty space

I woke up, you were gone
My soul abandoned, alone
If you had lingered on
The seed of hope would have grown

Why did you run from me
I loved and needed you so
What happened to make you flee
Please tell me, I need to know

Can I bring you back again

Can I ignite the fire once more

I beg you please my friend

Come walking back through my door

How I need your fire

Your intense desire

To inspire me like before

Oh sweet passion, please

Set my soul at ease

Fan the flames of my heart once more

Life is Good

Life is good, breathe it in
Realize that hope will win
Awaken from the dark embrace
And walk into a brighter place

So long this gloom and wretchedness
How wrong these wasted years
A song, a tune of blessedness
Rings strong within my ears

It's time to end this hopelessness
It's time to dry these tears
To cease from sorrow and distress
To cast away these fears

A different drink to savor
To quench this thirst within
Drink deeply this new flavor
And know that joy shall win

I Need a Fix

Inject me with joy

I need a fix

The energy bunny

Is all out of tricks

Give me a jolt

A pick-me-up smile

I'll bolt like a colt

And run for a while

It won't take much

My response will be swift

Just a gentle touch

To give me a lift ...

Next time you're low

It's certainly true

I hope you know

I'll do it for you

The Key

To those who think you know me

peering through the crack in my soul wall

peeping toms and janes

curiously wondering if I just might be insane

do you really know me at all

do you really care

or are you just standing gazing there

with the morbid desire

passing by the accident on the freeway

hoping to see a fatality

I want to give someone the key

the key to the real me

yet so often I cower in fear

that what you find will make you run and hide

repulsed by what you see inside

oh, for just one kindly passer-by

to stop and stay

not question why I cry

not run away

no matter what you see

willingly, unwaveringling, accept me

every mystery inside of me

to you, I would give the key

Shadow Boxing

I've spent a lifetime fighting shadows
I guess they call it shadow boxing
Swinging at the air

Futile attempts to vanquish the demons
Knock them cold and rendered helpless
Yet they were always there

Shadows, yet they are so real
I felt the pain of their every blow
But they felt nothing from me

These ghostly foes delivered such pain
And I their beaten victim fell
So broken, so void of mercy

I cannot defeat these enemies

Who have hidden themselves so expertly

They know no fear

So I befriended them one by one

Embraced them, learned each ones name

I drew them near

Someone told me to hold my friends close

But to hold my enemies closer

I decided to try

And the shadows who have inflicted pain

As I have begun to know each one

Have begun to die

Enigma

I'm an enigma,

a conflict of sorrow and pain,

yet sometimes I speak hope and faith ...

so often the pain wins out ...

but I feel like I need my pain, I crave the sorrow,

fear and doubt,

I need my sadness in some strange way ...

it inspires me to search for hope,

to believe that joy is possible

do I dare say I love my pain,

this paradox, this turmoil in my soul

do I dare proclaim,

I need the anguish, loneliness ...

so lost in a swirl of darkness,

a mingling of sadness and happiness ...

strange creature am I,

come glare at me in the carnival of souls,

a freakish enigma

Winter's Chill

There's a chill in the wintery night

Dogs barking across the way

A windless stillness, calm and cold

There's a chill in my wintery soul

Inside the furnace drones on

A rush of warm air and quietness

As my heart drones on with loneliness

There's a chill in my wintery soul

A fog drifts across my mind

Eyes close in sweet repose

Blissfully surrender my will

To escape from this wintery chill

Of Lonely Souls

I feel such an emptiness in my soul
It's an aching, lonely vacant hole
And nothing seems to fill it up
This drained and stained old coffee cup

I thought the thirst would go away
I filled and drank, but then today
The nagging, thirsting, unquenched pain
Was pounding in my heart again

In earthly or in heavenly realms
No one can take what overwhelms
My soul so steeped in desperation
Not even He who rules creation

For my soul is the only thing I own
And some places I must walk alone
And I think my God must understand
Sometimes I can't even hold His hand

And though this pain would break me down

And though some answers can't be found

And I cannot hear, or refuse to see

Perhaps someone will carry me

And perhaps someday in a better world

When across this dark abyss we're hurled

By an unseen force to a brighter day

All this lonely pain will fade away

And a higher purpose will take hold

Where warm and loving arms enfold

Where love is all that will be known

And souls will never feel alone

airborne virus

like an airborne virus spreading through a classroom

so contagious, infectious, a careless disease

indiscriminate, no one is immune

without antidote

without mercy

sorrow sweeps

all hope

all joy

under

the

heart's

rug

Spadina Street

One memorable night in Toronto

On Spadina Street or Yonge

A song arose inside me

A song I'd never sung

Amidst the crowds and revelry

It was something that you said

That what I sought was inside of me

It had never really fled

No one had stolen the pieces

I needed to make myself whole

But buried deep and hidden within

Lived the essence of my soul

"You have it", you said, "It's in you",

"What you need is inner-peace"

And on Spadina Street in Toronto

My soul found sweet release

Author's note:

1997: A true story of an awakening I desperately
needed, and how a friend's words changed my life.

The Fire of Life

In the lonely midnight hour I awaken, solitude surrounding me
But this is not a time of lonely pain or sorrow like before
I feel the warm and loving thoughts of days gone by abound in me
My heart so filled until I think it can hold nothing more

How I've missed this fullness in my soul, yet how I did not know
That this is what I've longed and hoped for all these lonely years
A primal quest for gentle tender comfort from so long ago
A deep abiding need for words to sooth my droning fears

How base and simple, had I known I would have cried so certainly
Yet I believed so many lies which suffocated, killed until
I did not see or realize the vastness of the hole inside of me
I thought that time would heal the sickness in my soul, my heart, my will

Alone and desperate, how we try so proudly to endure

Yet like a glowing ember separated from the flame

We only live a moment, shine so brightly, die for sure

When we could burn with warmth and cast away our every shame

Wisdom, love and truth have come to dwell, I don't know why

New strength has come to move me back into this fire so pure

When heart by heart and soul by soul just touching you and I

Can burn so very brightly with a fire that will endure

illusion

illusion of contentment

this smile, this mask

do you need to ask

it isn't real

it's not what I feel

don't you get it, this lie

it only hides the tears I cry

wiped away, hidden

true feelings are forbidden

behind the wall I've built inside

the illusion of truth

kept outside

under lock and key

no one can see

the turmoil locked

in the soul of me

demented confusion

contented delusion

it's all an illusion

just let me be

Losing You

I keep losing you,
   Or is it me who's wandering
   Lost in forest dreams
I try to leave a breadcrumb trail
   To lead me home to you again
Doubt-birds seem to eat them all
 So this forest holds me in
But now and then I hear mockingbirds
They seem to sing familiar words
   Words of me
   Songs of you
   Your words too
   Love-lyrics lead me back to you
Out of dark and lonesome woods
   Into the light of day
When across a sunny meadow
 I catch a glimpse of you ...
... As you run away
 So confusing, when ...
I'm losing you ... again

A Place of Peace

A Place of Peace
Is where I've wanted to be
Where calmness and delight prevail
And nothing frightens me

I bask in the warmth of gentleness
Like the glow of the noonday sun
And in this blissful drowsiness
With sleep I'm overcome

Rest, my child, slumber and dream
May every sorrow cease
May joy spring forth, a gushing stream
As you awaken again in peace

And if you stray into turmoil

Or walk into a darker place

Let your heart and stride just recoil

And turn to never miss a pace

For power comes with determination

Rise up, turn around, and run

Return to the sure elation

That's offered to everyone

Your life is a gift, receive it

And love, is from God, believe it

Let Him give you a sweet release

In the arms of the Prince of Peace

Storms

My day, my life, has been a storm
A tempest overwhelming
Dragging me beneath the waves
Till I feel I'm drowning ...

Where is a rescuer who cares
Who sees me in my plight?
Then you appeared and reached to me
And pulled me to the light

A gentle word, a tender touch
A friendly smile, a breath of life
How kind, how lovingly you came
To cast away my strife

And for a moment all is well
The tempest calms, peace is repaired
And hope is reachable once more
Because you came ... and cared

Wayward Soul

Floating on the winds
Countless wayward souls
Lonely lost and aching
Defective hearts with holes

Many hearts are breaking
Sometimes one heart is mine
A cruel thief is taking
What little joy I find

Perhaps this endless sorrow
Will fade through fitful sleep
A glimmer of hope tomorrow
A reason not to weep

Oh wistful winds please cease
Release my captive soul
Replace my pain with peace
My broken heart console

In My Dream

You were in my dream

I found you waiting there

You were so serene

Lounging in a chair

The joy I felt when I saw you

Was so very wonderful

I smiled and sat beside you

And said, "Hello Beautiful"

It seems even in my dreams

Even there I adore you

You fill my empty soul

You thrill my lonely heart

Stay near me I implore you

Whether sleeping or awake

I long for more of you

You take away the ache

You make my heart feel new

In my day

In my night

In my dreams

Within my sight

Seeing you

Being with you

Feels so right ...

If Only

If only ...

perhaps the saddest words

ever spoken

there is such truth behind them

two words that speak

of promises broken

hearts in turmoil

ancient fears

uncried tears

the mantra of the lonely

an excuse that wilts the soul

imprisoning the heart

two words we speak in haste

if only ...

these two words ...

could be erased

solitude and silence

I sometimes seek solitude and silence

perfect peace on a glassy sea

where all is calm and quietness

and the whisper of a sacred psalm

as a gentle breeze washes over me

in these moments when all seems right

the eyes of my soul awaken to new sight

reflecting truth once obscured by night

a mirror of light upon the silent sea

Yet there is a time for solitude to cease

when winds increase and waves arise

a tidal surge as loneliness cries

white cap warnings splash upon the heart

silence breaks and rushes to the shore

I seek the touch of a warm embrace

a knowing glance, a welcome face

and smiles that speak a thousand words

kindness overwhelming, love so pure

solitude and silence

kindred souls and kindness

a delicate dance

my universe in balance

Huggers of the Soul

Some people blunder and plod through life
Untouched by the depths of the spirit
So blind yet they think they see clearly
When truth speaks they seldom hear it

Some people trudge along so burdened
So enslaved yet they think they're free
So happy without, yet tortured within
When light shines they seldom see

Some people hug the body
And cherish a temporal goal
Yet amidst this vast and dying crowd
Some people hug the soul

There's a poison infesting my mind and heart
There's a pain beyond control
Please send a soothing, healing balm
A hugger of my soul ...

I'm Here

I'm here

in my swirl of loneliness,

dizzy, sometimes drowning,

sometimes catching a breath

my head above the waves ...

waiting for someone to visit me,

in my dreams,

in my soul ...

wishing,

hoping,

wanting ...

gasping

  for

   one

    more

     breath

I Love My Life

I love my life, my life is good

Even when I feel misunderstood

I've come to see and realize

That joy sometimes comes in disguise

And when the pain seems hard to bear

And when nobody seems to care

Tears wash my eyes and cleanse my soul

And help me see a nobler goal

For without struggles, strife and pain

How could my life move forward, gain

The higher place I need to be

And flowers bloom inside of me

Pain only makes the joy so sweet

And sorrow gives me swifter feet

To run with laughter in this race

And lets my heart receive more grace

I love my life, much love abounds

Listen, hear this joy I've found

Take, eat this overwhelming fruit

And join me in this great pursuit

Prolific

Prolific

That's what I want to be

This is no trick

I want you to know the real me

I want my words to reveal

Perfectly and freely

Who I am, my joys and sorrows

My dark past

And my lost tomorrows

Yet somehow

Through the words I speak

My soul spills out

And I realize my life is not that bleak

My imperfections are a part of me

I can love the broken heart in me

For the truth I seek is found in you too

All it takes is a moment of honesty

For me to really know you

Then perhaps it could be

The way I could really and truly know me

And in the give and take

In the take and give

Maybe this is the way

We were all meant to live

Maybe this is purpose and hope

And meaning

Maybe this is life and love

And being

Prolific

Is what I want to be

It is no trick

To let you know the real me

Lock the Door

I felt a moment of sorrow
However it was fleeting
A strength arose inside me
My heart intensely beating

I spoke firmly to this sorrow
It was of my childhood born
So ancient and so long ago
No reason now to mourn

A twinge of age-old pain
So easily awakening
Would steal my joy away
All my happiness taking

I sent this sorrow away
It can't harm me anymore
There shall be no sadness today
And then I locked the door

Something About You

There's something so pleasant about you
That always draws me in
Something mysterious, intangible
I just don't know where to begin

But it tastes like sweetest nectar
From a thousand honey bees
And it sounds like children's laughter
That sets our hearts at ease

The fragrance of a garden of flowers
Aromas of a Summer day
Your voice like soothing showers
Washes my cares away

There are so many things about you
Words fail me to completely express
Everything you say, everything you do
Brings me such happiness

Catharsis of Poetry

What tyranny is this lonely sorrow

this desperation drawing me

to seek another broken heart

It seems to be that poetry

springs forth with greatest beauty

from the depths of deepest pain

So commonly it is often said

that opposites attract, I disagree.

The premise seems more clear to me

that sorrow is the key.

I search for similar pain

reflected back to me.

I'm thankful for my pain and sorrow

It makes me dig more deeply

and from the depths of my soul

springs forth more meaningful poetry.

Poetry born of pain

fits my soul like a glove,

and my hands and heart ...

are warmed by love.

Sunny Rain

Sunny outside

Sad inside

Friends dog died

Reminded me of last year

When my Annie was still here

No more barking nights

No more playful canine delights

I remember how I cried

Some hurts don't easily subside

Smile ... Sunny today and tomorrow

While in my heart ...

　　　It's raining sorrow

The Truth of Me

Some people cry
pour out their heart
speak their mind
display emotions
clearly ... blatantly

Some people sigh
a subtle soft sound
true feelings hard to find
hurt ... buried underground
their eyes remain dry

Some people laugh

but it's a lie

a cover ... just an alibi

a mask to hide the sadness

pretense of gladness ...

this is so hollow

I choose the solace of sorrow

to feel what is real

to know the truth of me

this is why I choose to cry

only then is my soul free

Kindred Soul

Sometimes I hurt yet cannot cry

Sometimes I feel an aching

A loneliness, a pain so deep

Till my heart feels it's breaking

Sometimes I cannot find my soul

Sometimes alone and weary

A sadness grips, so firmly holds

My heart so lost and dreary

Sometimes I cannot find the words

Sometimes I cannot speak

Or tell the hurting of my soul

My wounded heart so bleak

Sometimes hearts meet and sing

And souls enfold perchance

Or by some high design

Some spirits learn to dance

Sometimes amidst the turmoil

While facing painful choices

When touched by a kindred soul

My wandering soul rejoices

One Desire

If I could only hear her voice
Breathe softly in my ear
To feel that tingling sensation
Just to have her near

The words she says won't matter
My senses would ignite
My blanket arms would enfold her
And hold her through the night

She lights my soul on fire
Just imagining her here
She awakens my one desire
Breathing softly in my ear

Blissful Butterfly

Floating through my mind
A wistful butterfly
Delicate and frail
Upon a breeze you sail

Blissful, Beautiful
Entrancing, Mesmerizing
Fleeting Free and Graceful
Making my heart sing

Lift my cares away
Teach me how to fly
Into a brighter day
Blissful Butterfly

Sometimes Sadness

Sometimes sadness floats across the sky
Have you felt this, seen it happen too
Have you ever wondered why
As seasons change the storms appear, subside
And reasons allude our understanding
Sometimes the clouds must cry

The sorrows of the world evaporate
Gather in the atmosphere, accumulate
Just like the lakes and oceans do
   Until the weight is overwhelming,
   Showers fall, the rain of pain
   Disperses to us all
Yes ... Sometimes the sadness
   That we feel perplexes, vexes us,
   Just seems to have no reason

We wonder and ask why ...
Perhaps it is the sorrow floating in the sky
Sometimes sadness is the cloudburst of the world ...
   We all must cry

Frozen Emotion

paralyzed, moving in slow motion

feels like frozen emotion

lack of motivation, enthusiasm gone

not wanting to move, unable to go on

not wanting ... anything

lost in a maze, wandering

sad, too tired to be confused

drifting, existing, riding a tide

joy refused, confused, must hide

lonely, wanting only to cry

hoping, seeking, wondering why

purpose unclear, riddled with fear

yet too sad to be afraid ...

too afraid to be angry ...

thoughts of happiness fade

emptiness within and around me

paralyzed and floating in my mind

adrift in my soul's ocean

sometimes life seems so unkind

so very cold ... this frozen emotion

soul flowers

loneliness, is like gasping for air

your voice like oxygen

lifts me from despair

my once heavy heart

now weightless, takes wing

soaring, floating through my soul space

with just the vision

the memory of your face

your smile inspires me to sing

remedy for every longing

you are like Spring showers

drenching my earth

where seeds of loneliness

now give birth to flowers

of happiness ...

how wonderful to finally know

this is how soul flowers grow ...

my life

my life moves on towards the inevitable end

I hope before then I can fill it up with some joy

there seems to be a deficit of laughter

and an overabundance of sadness

maybe I can find a coupon for a discount on gladness

I would even pay full price

just a simple smile would be so nice

I have always heard that attitude is everything

but sometimes life just slaps you down

steals away the reason to sing

maybe if I get my guitar and start to play

the music will carry some of this sorrow away

and I'll try my best to avoid the sad country songs

it would just be nice if I had someone to sing along

Sorrow Floats

Sometimes my sorrow floats away

I don't know how or why

Sometimes I laugh

Sometimes I cry

Perhaps this proves I'm still alive

For this I shall rejoice

Sometimes I realize joy is a choice

As sorrow floats away into the sky

Sometimes ...

Tempests

Tempests toss my soul
As on a storm-raged sea
A ship amidst the waves
How lost I seem to be

And washed upon a shore
A barren, lonely land
I wander through the night
With none to hold my hand

And surging deep within
My heart is gripped in darkness
Alone in desolation
Shipwrecked amidst the bleakness

Wandering and weary
Hopeless beyond control
Wounded, ravaged, dreary
Tempests toss my soul

Tormented Soul

Sad Empty Tormented Soul
Why must you feel this way
Lost and Alone
All that you've known
Only Despair today
It won't go away

Fearful Wounded Child Inside
Why must you hide this way
Afraid to cry
Or whimper, you sigh
Invisible You fade away
Why can't you come out and play

Soul Quake

Three thirty-three

Wide awake

Seems to be

Another soul quake

Remembering

A few things said

Minor tremors

In my head

Thoughts like thunder

Roll around

Fitful sleep

Unstable ground

Tensions tremble

Sensations shake

Three thirty-three

Wide awake

uninspired

uninspired ...

in a place between

  night and day

my world is gray

scattered remnants

my soul a dismal disarray

colors faded, blended

hope degraded, ended

overshadowed, shaded

uninspired ...

not much left to say

my world ...

so very ...

gray

My Year of Tears

I've had many years of laughter, many years of joy
But this has been my year of greatest pain

My brother in his grave, my father in the home
My mother in her anguish ... I feel so alone

My children are my joy, my parents are my pain
I'm torn between two worlds ... life will never be the same

This hurt is not despair, yet deep and unrelenting
This aching of my soul seems over-whelming, never-ending

Yet my faith has not been shaken, I do not ask Him why
I don't deserve the comfort that He alone provides

I look to Him for hope, He shares my deepest pain
No one on earth can understand or lift my soul again

I cry to Him in sorrow, He feels my greatest woe
I comprehend His love for me that everyone should know

Drifting

Floating, drifting on a sadness sea
Tides and currents carry me
Distant far away from shore
Never to return anymore

Carried along by whims of wind
Rising, falling to rise again
Somehow calm within this place
Peaceful in the wave's embrace

Rudder, sails - broken, gone
Strange mercy as I travel on
Drifting on this endless sea
Unsure where it carries me

No cause for worry or distress
I've redefined my happiness
So many things beyond my power
I live my life from hour to hour

Let go of people, places, things
Unburdened I can spread new wings
My soul can fly, my heart can soar
Where none can harm me anymore

Author's Biography

Jerry Caspell thinks of himself first as a Poet. Although organically shy, he loves writing Poetry to express his deepest feelings. These are very personal and sacred to him. Jerry has had a lifetime goal to publish his poetry, and now, he has made that dream a reality, with Elusive Butterfly.

Secondly, Jerry is a singer/songwriter. He has made an album of his original songs which you can find on Amazon called Soul Reflections. You can also purchase Jerry's album on iTunes.

Made in the USA
Coppell, TX
19 January 2021